"All over this nation, God is stirring the hearts of men to rise up and enter into their God-given destiny. Lou Turner's lifelong passion is to see men enter into their divine purpose in life. 'Living Life God's Way,' of which this book is a part, is born out of this passion. Throughout this Bible study series, Turner opens up God's Word to help you discover HIS plan for your success in your life, family, and work. If you are ready to get off the treadmill, to begin to enjoy God's fullness in your life and make a significant contribution to the world around you, I recommend that you dive into this life-transforming Bible study."

Hal H. Sacks, D.Min., *BridgeBuilders International Leadership Network*

"It seems North American culture is rapidly moving toward what the Bible calls 'everyone doing what is right in his own mind' (Judges 21:25). The prophet Isaiah declared, 'Woe to those who call evil, good, and good, evil' (Isaiah 5:20). This Bible study series will challenge every man in the 21st century as 'iron sharpens iron'! The Q&As at the end of each chapter really personalize the teaching."

Dennis Conner, *Co-Founder/President, Called to Serve Prayer-Coaching Ministry*

"I have known Lou Turner for over twenty years. Lou loves Jesus and has built his life on the Word of God. Lou's Bible study series, 'Living Life God's Way,' is full of biblical truth that has been tested and can be applied by disciples of Jesus in practical ways. These books will help you grow in your faith and gain confidence and competence, which will increase your fruitfulness in Christ."

Mark Buckley, *Founding Pastor of Living Streams Church*

Living Life God's Way

A Man's Work and Ministry

Lou Turner

A Man's Work and Ministry
First Edition, 2020
Copyright © 2020 by Lou Turner

A Man's Work and Ministry is part of the Living Life God's Way Series by Lou Turner.

All rights reserved. No part of this publication may be reproduced, stored in a retrieval system, or transmitted in any form by any means—electronic, mechanical, photocopy, recording, or otherwise—except for brief quotations in critical reviews or articles, without the prior permission of the author, except as provided by U.S. copyright law.

Scriptures taken from the New King James Version®, copyright © 1982 by Thomas Nelson. Used by permission. All rights reserved.

Scriptures taken from the Holy Bible, New International Version®, NIV®, copyright © 1973, 1978, 1984, 2011 by Biblica, Inc.™ Used by permission of Zondervan. All rights reserved worldwide. www.zondervan.com The "NIV" and "New International Version" are trademarks registered in the United States Patent and Trademark Office by Biblica, Inc.™

Some of the anecdotal illustrations in this book are true to life and are included with the permission of the persons involved. All other illustrations are composites of real situations, and any resemblance to people living or dead is coincidental.

To order additional books:
www.amazon.com
www.hislifeinus.com

ISBN-13: 978-1-7329092-5-0

Editorial and Book Packaging: Inspira Literary Solutions, Gig Harbor, WA
Book Design: PerfecType, Nashville, TN
Cover Design: MTWdesign, Dickson, TN
Printed in the USA by Ingram Spark

He will be like a tree firmly planted by streams of water,
Which yields its fruit in its season
And its leaf does not wither;
And in whatever he does, he prospers.

Psalm 1:3

TABLE OF CONTENTS

Preface ix

How to Use this Book xi

Introduction to A Man's Work and Ministry xiii

1. God Meant Man to Work 1

2. God Shapes a Man through Work 15

3. Life on the Job 27

4. A Man's Work Is Integral to His Ministry 37

A Final Word 53

About the Author 55

PREFACE

We live in a world that has largely forgotten what manhood is about. In the Western world, men are often portrayed on television as buffoons who are out of touch and must rely on their wives to straighten them out. These characters are portrayed as silly, insensitive, lacking common sense, and when they do speak, they are generally wrong. They are usually portrayed as either ridiculously weak or overly macho. They are not able to commit to a long-term relationship and often mistreat women. Positive role models are hard to find in the media.

However, the Bible teaches a different type of manhood, the authentic one. Men are to be leaders, loving their wives and children, excelling in their work, and standing for truth. They are to be men of wisdom, knowledge, having godly character and seeking after God and His direction. They are to be exhibiting godly leadership at church, in the community, and in business, and to be a light to those around them. They are to be men of compassion and love, as well as courageous and bold when needed.

Men go astray from these ideals, including Christian men, due to improper convictions or beliefs about life. They have received these from various sources: well-meaning family and friends, the media, and the culture around them—a world system that promotes the tearing down of God's biblical truths.

But without proper biblical foundation, we will all go astray.

PREFACE

That's why I wrote these books, containing insights, observations, and biblical truths distilled over the course of my decades of life and ministry. Each section is designed to be a stand-alone section for study and consideration. I hope this series, *Living Life God's Way*, will be used to disciple men in biblical truths for life. Whether you use it for yourself, with a group, or to mentor or disciple someone else, my hope is that it will be a blessing to you and encourage you to seek God and grow in Him.

HOW TO USE THIS BOOK

What does it mean to be a "good" husband and father?
How do I live out the Christian life at work?
What does God want from me—and how am I supposed to find that out?

These were questions that plagued me as a young man—questions, I learned, that are at the front of many men's minds at various times in their lives. For me, these questions began my quest to seek God and discover the answers I needed. My discoveries, over the years of my life, led to this series of booklets, *Living Life God's Way*. While I do not suggest that I have discovered all of the answers, my desire is to share what I have learned and hope it will be helpful for you. This series discusses 13 topics that every man must deal with, regardless of his work, calling, profession, or circumstances. It is difficult to know how to live the Christian life without understanding what God says about these areas of life.

These topics are:

1. Seeking and Finding God
2. Who You Are in Christ
3. A Man's Work and Ministry
4. Understanding Authority
5. A Man and His Wife

HOW TO USE THIS BOOK

6. A Man and His Children
7. Getting Guidance from God
8. Overcoming Strongholds
9. A Man and Money
10. Repentance, Forgiveness, and Restitution
11. Being a Leader
12. A Man and Sex
13. The Test of Pride

You can use these books to study on your own, in a small group, or with a larger group of men. Each topic or booklet is a stand-alone study, and a person can begin with any one he chooses. They are different lengths and can be adapted to various settings—home, church, or community—all topics that are pertinent to today.

Explore what the Bible says about these important and critical areas of life. The encouragement is to read these with an open heart, asking God to reveal His truth to you in each of these areas. Pray that His Spirit will show you His truth, so that you may live in it and enjoy all God has for you. I pray that you experience the blessing and presence of God in your life as you draw closer to Him and become more aware of His leading in every area of your life.

INTRODUCTION TO A MAN'S WORK AND MINISTRY

Whether he excels or coasts, works hard or takes it easy, work is integral to a man. For most men, work is a priority. They generally work eight to ten hours a day, five days a week, for the majority of their most productive years. Their energy and even possibly their hopes and dreams are involved in their work. In fact, it helps define who they are and what purpose they serve.

Ask a man who he is, and he will often reply by telling you the type of work he does. Ask a man to talk about his life, and he will often mention his work and what he has accomplished. Right or wrong, the majority of men define themselves this way. Since they work most of their adult lives, their feeling of fulfillment and success is closely tied to what they accomplish in their work. Were they successful? Did they advance?

Work is an important and God-given activity. In this study we will see that God wants to be vitally involved in our work, and to work through us as we minister to others in our work.

Chapter 1
God Meant Man to Work

As the Bible opens in the first chapter of Genesis, we see God working to create a magnificent world for us to live in. At the end of His work, the Bible says, *"God saw everything that he had made, and behold, it was very good"* (Genesis 1:31). As we read this, we sense that God felt satisfaction in seeing His creation. He looked at all He had done and said, "It was very good."

I am personally awed as I take time to behold God's creation and think about its complexity and how magnificent and beautiful it is. I must admit I don't understand all God did, but I greatly appreciate His creation. I can't even imagine what the new heavens and new earth spoken of in Revelation will be like!

We are made in God's image, and part of that design is both the need and desire to work and be productive. We have an innate need to work, and to feel successful or productive in our work.

A MAN'S WORK AND MINISTRY

God created us this way; work is part of the way we express who we are. In fact, work is a gift from God. I believe God put in all of us a need to be productive. When we don't do that, or stop doing it, I think we begin to die inside. We all need to be productive in some way.

Through work we are productive. We produce, invent, provide, accomplish, build societies, and supply for our needs and the needs of others. We build buildings, roads, and machines, and improve our standard of living. In all of this activity, we are to glorify God in the way we go about it and accomplish it. As we work and seek God, He gives us ideas, solutions to problems, ways to accomplish things, direction in life, and He promises to bless our work as we seek Him. God intended all of us to work, be productive, and accomplish things. He gave us varying gifts, talents, and abilities to use to do this.

I got my first job when I was fourteen, and started buying my own clothes and providing my own spending money. I have worked ever since. I have never regretted this, as it taught me to work and provide for myself through my work.

I always assumed I would have to work when I went away to college. I got jobs during the school year and worked full time over the summer. The summer between my freshman and sophomore year, my roommate and I were both looking for jobs. We found work at a garbage collection company that paid more than other jobs we looked into, so we took it and became garbage men. They put us on a garbage truck together, and we worked hard, but also had fun. Back then, you had to pick up the garbage can manually and dump it into the hopper of the truck. So, we took turns driving and "dumping." In college, you do what you need to do to get by.

Since then, I have worked for others and have worked for myself. I have been privileged to have senior management positions in national and international companies and to see God bless my efforts. I have also worked for myself and started new ventures. I have been through periods when everything I touched seemed to be blessed, and times where nothing seemed to work out, no matter what I did.

I've had jobs I loved and jobs that were difficult. Work has been a big part of my life and a major part of how God has shaped me, revealed Himself, molded me, changed me, and used me to influence and benefit others. He has revealed Himself to me through my work. I have discovered God's faithfulness, His provision, and His guidance and leadership through my work. God has worked through my work environment to develop character and change me. That was all part of His design. Biblically, work is one of the priorities of a man's life.

God Gave Man Work

Genesis 2 notes that after God created the earth, *"no bush of the field was yet in the land and no small plant of the field had yet sprung up—for the LORD God had not caused it to rain on the land, and **there was no man to work the ground**"* (verse 5, emphasis mine). Obviously, God intended man to work on the earth. He was to care for the place where God had placed him.

The account goes on to describe how the Lord established work for man: *"Then the Lord took the man and put him in the Garden of Eden to tend and keep it"* (Genesis 2:15). God made a special place for man on earth—the Garden of Eden—and gave man a special task: tend the garden. God knew everything about the man he had created, and He knew that man needed purpose and work to feel productive. Though man's work was made more difficult as a result of sin (Genesis 3:17-18), work itself was not a result of sin.

God gave work to man and He uses work as a means to give man creativity and expression, to use his talents and abilities, to provide for needs, to bless others, and to find purpose and meaning.

Work Is an Avenue for Creativity

Work is where we can create and achieve dreams. God's creation of the world was the ultimate height of work and creativity. God took great pleasure in His creation. We know this, because Genesis 1:31 says, *"Then God saw everything that He had made, and indeed it was very good."* Since we are made in God's image, it is only natural that we, too, should want to take satisfaction in our work. The writer of Ecclesiastes talked of this: *"There is nothing better for a man than that he should eat and drink, and that his soul should enjoy good in his labor. This also, I say, was from the hand of God"* (Ecclesiastes 2:24).

Regardless of a man's talents, aptitudes, or spiritual gifts, there are a multitude of ways he can express himself through his work. My wife, Joan, is an artist and interior decorator. I am constantly amazed at her talent and creativity. However, creativity is not limited to the work of an artist, musician, writer, or inventor. I don't have artistic creativity. In fact, when I try to draw no one seems to know what it is. But I do enjoy being creative in my tasks. When I find a creative solution to a problem, I feel a great sense of fulfillment.

Creativity can find expression in any aspect of work. Finding a way to do a job better, taking joy in doing a job well, determining to be a source of encouragement to those around us, taking initiative to get things done before you are asked, doing things to the best of your ability—these are all ways to be diligent and show creativity in your work.

If we find our work dull or boring, we need to ask God to change our hearts toward our work and seek Him to get involved in our work with us. We also need to ask God to open our hearts and eyes to see how He views our work. Either God will change our attitude toward our work, or ultimately He will open a door to an area of work where we can find satisfaction and personal expression.

Whether we work for another or for ourselves, we can express ourselves, be creative, and make the most of our work as unto the Lord. I have had some of my best and most fruitful life experiences working for others. Learning to manage others, learning the synergy and creativity of a team of people dedicated to the same goal, praying and asking God for solutions, and seeing Him get involved in my work have truly been life changing.

Work Provides for Our Family's Needs

Scripture also teaches that a man is to work to provide for the normal needs we all have. The Apostle Paul reminded the church in Thessalonica to *"aspire to lead a quiet life, to mind your own business, and to work with your own hands, as we commanded you"* (1 Thessalonians 4:11). When he wrote again, he emphasized the point:

> *For even when we were with you, we commanded you this: If anyone will not work, neither shall he eat. For we hear that there are some who walk among you in a disorderly manner, not working at all, but are busybodies. Now those who are such we command and exhort through our Lord Jesus Christ that they work in quietness and eat their own bread.* (2 Thessalonians 3:10-12, emphasis mine)

It is clear that work is the route through which we provide for our needs.

In addition, our work provides for our family members. The early church provided for widows with no family, but for others, the children or grandchildren were to *"make some return to their parents, for this is pleasing in the sight of God."* The passage gets even stronger: *"But if anyone does not provide for his own, and especially for those of his household, he has denied the faith and is worse than an unbeliever"* (1 Timothy 5:8). There is no question that as men we are called to work and to provide for our households. (First Timothy 5:8 speaks in the masculine and is talking primarily to men. But this applies to both men and women.)

Men are to work to provide for themselves and their families. Many women are single moms and must provide for themselves and their children. It can be a daunting task to have to work full time and take care of children when there is no one to help. But God sees this and is prepared to help single moms when they seek Him and cry out to Him for help.

For both men and women, working to provide for themselves and their families is both a privilege and a sacrifice. We got married when I was a junior in college. When we married, Joan worked full time and I worked part time while I was in school. We had to provide for ourselves. Neither of our families were able to help us financially and, frankly, we did not expect it. We accepted this and did not think it was a hardship to have to work to provide for ourselves. After college we had children, and we had to make a decision about raising our children. For a time we both worked. But we came to believe it was best for Joan to stay at home to take care of our children and provide a loving, nurturing home. So, I had to believe God to provide through me.

There were some lean and challenging times at first as I was getting established in my work. But God was faithful. I loved coming home at night to our children and the home Joan made for us. My work made it possible for her to work at home, caring for our children. I considered it my responsibility to support and provide for my family, whom God gave me.

It also meant sacrifice. There were times when things were tough. At times I have loved my work and looked forward to going to work. At other times I have found myself in difficult working situations and wished I could make a change. But I knew I had to work to provide for my family; there was no other choice. So I went to work and believed God to help me and direct me in all work situations. The difficult circumstances became a learning and growing situation. I had to change my attitudes and I spent time on my knees asking for His direction and help in my work. God definitely used the workplace to change me, develop character in me, and bring me to trust Him to bless my work.

One Christmas when our children were young, we had little money for gifts. So Joan and I decided we would buy gifts for our children and nothing for each other. They were young (two, four, and six), and so did not expect a lot. But God provided for Joan and me also. A man in our church found out that we did not have money to buy gifts for each other and bought gifts for us so we could have Christmas gifts. We were blessed, surprised, and thankful. The gifts were nicer than we would have bought or could have afforded!

I had to learn to honor Joan's contribution to our family as she worked at home. I had to learn to make her feel valued, something I did not always do well. I didn't always show the level of respect for her work at home as I should have. She sacrificed for our family. When my oldest daughter was a cheerleader, Joan was the cheerleaders' sponsor. She drove them places and was at every game, supporting our daughter and ministering to the squad. When our younger daughter was in Brownies, then Girl Scouts, then high school volleyball, Joan was always there to support her. She made our children feel loved and valued—and often did a better job at it than I did.

As men, we need to ask what is best for our families and our children. It says in Malachi 2:15, "*Has not the Lord made them one? In flesh and spirit they are His. And why one? Because he was seeking godly offspring. So guard yourself in your spirit, and do not break faith with the wife of your youth."* God desires us to have a family that seeks Him and honors Him in their lives. As men, we are to be priests in our home and encourage our wife and children to seek Him and trust in Him. Working just to have more stuff is not the answer. But being sensitive to what is best for our family is very important and something we should seek the Lord about.

The questions to consider are these: 1) what is best for your family life and the children? 2) what is God's will for your family? Certainly, a strong marriage and a strong family are God's will and best for any family. Once we have children, God wants us to "raise up a godly offspring" (Malachi 2:15). Loving them, teaching and training them to seek God and have godly character—those are things we can't leave to others. They are our responsibility.

For men, this means we must be willing to use our work and income to provide for our family. We must also manage our desires and lifestyle expectations so that our income can cover our family's needs. Every couple should develop a family culture that honors God. Praying and seeking God for His plan for your family is important. Our families are a trust from God and we want to lead as He would have us to.

Ask God to give you wisdom for leading your family. Pray with your wife regularly for your marriage and children (if you have them), and ask God for insight into His will for your marriage and family.

I fully realize there are men who either cannot work or are limited by physical handicaps. Many of our veterans have come home with limbs gone or other limitations. These men still have much to offer and can find ways to be productive. In many of these cases, their wives must shoulder part or much of the load. However, God is aware of their situations and as they turn to Him and seek Him, He will help them and show them ways they can be productive. He promises to provide for all His children, not just some.

God wants us to seek Him for His provision. He will reveal His will to us, the path we are to take, and the opportunities He has for us, as we seek Him. Remember, God is faithful. Working and providing for one's family is God's calling to men and women. God doesn't expect you to do this on your own. He promises to be with you, to lead you, and to provide for you and your family. Open your life to Him and expect to see Him working on your behalf. Ask God to help you and to show you and your wife creative ways to make this happen. Life and work provide a great adventure in faith.

We should pray and believe God for His best for us, our marriage, and our family.

Work Increases Fulfillment

Along with expressing our creativity and supplying our needs, when a man works hard, sees the fruit of his labor, and experiences success, it gives him confidence and a feeling of purpose.

Most men want to succeed in their efforts at work and take pride in what they have accomplished. They are motivated to provide a meaningful product or service for others, and they get a great deal of satisfaction in doing this. Inventors and entrepreneurs are often motivated by this desire. Many dream of having their own companies or working for themselves. This can be a Godly desire, especially if the product or service benefits and helps the welfare of others.

There is both a positive and negative side to this drive to succeed. The desire for our work to prosper is from God—that's the positive. However, like all of God's gifts, it can become warped and turn into a driving passion. That's the negative. Many men will stop at nothing to succeed—and watch out for those who get in their way!

Our work must not become the end goal, but rather a part of our lives. We must realize that no matter what we accomplish on Earth, only a personal relationship with God can bring true and complete fulfillment. Being diligent and working hard, to the best of our ability, is important. We should want to do as well in our work as we can. But it is also important to spend time with our family. We need to know when to shut down work and focus on them. Our wives need a husband and our children need a father.

We labor here in faith with the tasks God has given us to do. We can take pleasure in seeing success in our activities because we realize any success is because of His blessing. Doing well at work that one is well-suited for is a great combination that brings a sense of accomplishment and a level of fulfillment. However, if we expect to be completely fulfilled by what we do here on Earth, we will be disappointed. In this life, we will always be looking forward to our life with God and being in His presence.

> *For we know that the whole creation groans and labors with birth pangs together until now. And not only they, but we also who have the first fruits of the Spirit, even we ourselves groan within ourselves, eagerly waiting for the adoption, the redemption of our body. (Romans 8:23)*

Only our relationship with God can bring true fulfillment. God made us to need Him. When we leave Him out of our life, or don't give Him the proper place in our life that He deserves, we will always sense that we are lacking something in our life.

No matter how successful we are or what we accomplish, we need a relationship with God to satisfy our soul. He wants to be intimately involved in our life in all areas, including our work. There is a natural hunger in us for Him. If we neglect seeking Him, the hunger goes on and most will try to satisfy it in other ways. Work, success, sex, sports, money, or power will not replace the need we have for God in our life. If we neglect our relationship with Him, we will always feel we are missing something. We are: we are missing our relationship with God.

Here on Earth, we are "groaning" and waiting. Since we are creatures comprised of body, soul, and spirit, fulfillment can only come when all facets of our person are complete. We will be incomplete until we are with the Lord. But while we are here, God has work for us to do, yet we must keep it in perspective. However, our relationship with Him is what our soul and spirit long for.

I was speaking with a wealthy man one day, and asked him, "Ten years after you have died, how many people will remember you? Of those who do, how often will they think of you? And when they do think or speak of you, what will they say and how will they remember you?"

He became very quiet as he thought of this. He looked at me and said, "That's not a very encouraging thought."

"I know," I answered, "but it is reality."

A Godly Perspective of Work

The drive to succeed must not be stronger than the desire to please God. As we learn to order our priorities according to God's priorities, God will bless our work and His peace and purposes can then come into the middle of our endeavors.

We should pray over our work and try to honor God in all we do. Our attitudes, our work ethic, our diligence, and the way we treat others will speak volumes to those around us. Our life is a living testament played out before others.

My brother-in-law was a great man. He had a gentle nature, a great sense of humor, worked hard, and was reliable and honest in all of his dealings. He was a union journeyman pipe fitter for years and then became an estimator for a construction company. He loved the Lord and his family, and treated others with respect. He was not a rich man financially. But when he was killed in an auto accident, the church was packed at his funeral. Most who attended were not just from his church, but those who knew him and dealt with him in business. I was amazed at the respect others had for him. He was well thought of and lived his life in a manner honoring to the Lord. I hope I have half as many at my funeral!

When we begin to realize that God gave us work, that He wants to be involved in it, that He wants to reveal Himself to us in and through our work, all of a sudden our work looks entirely different. It becomes an expression of our life to God. *"And whatever you do,"* Colossians 3:23 says, *"do it heartily, as to the Lord and not to men, knowing that from the Lord you will receive the reward of the inheritance; for you serve the Lord Christ."* Since God gave us work to do, it is an act of service to Him. Honoring God in our work becomes an act of worship.

> *Getting God involved in our work is the difference between "just working" and seeing our work and its activity as an outlet for God's Spirit to express Himself through us.*

QUESTIONS FOR REFLECTION AND DISCUSSION

1. Do you see work as a positive activity in your life? If so, how?

   _____
   _____
   _____
   _____

2. Do you see your family as a trust from God? Do you realize your role in the home is important?

___

___

___

3. Consider what it looks like to conduct your work life in a godly manner. Godly people intend to please God or honor Him in all of life. They practice honesty and integrity, pray, are teachable, and actively apply biblical truths to all of life. In general, they align their behavior with God's principles, and truth. However, godly people are not perfect. They fail and make mistakes. Write below what your work means to you.

___

___

___

___

Below, write out how you practice godliness on the job.

___

___

___

4. On an average day, do you view your work as God-given? If that's not something you often think about, how might doing so change a normal workday for you?

5. Do you feel like your work is blessed of God? If so, state why. If not, state why.

TAKE A KNEE

Let's pray by bowing before our Father. If you are unable to kneel, then bow before Him in your heart. *"Dear Father, Your Word tells me that You have ordained work. Help me to view my work as You do. Make me aware of how You want to be involved in my work life and work through me to others. Show me how to be creative and productive in my work as I work to provide for myself and my family. Father, I want Your will for me, my wife, and my family. Please reveal Your best for us in this area. Make my attitudes toward my work as You would have them to be. Grant me the fulfillment You want to give me through it. Bless my work and help me to grow, learn, develop character, and be successful in it."*

Chapter 2

God Shapes a Man through Work

Jim was a committed Christian man. He loved his family, his church, and the Lord. However, he was driven by a passion to succeed.

His parents had been in ministry all of their lives and had failed to provide for their retirement. Now, in their old age, they had no income and were completely dependent on others.

Jim was determined he would not end up like his parents. He feared failure and not having his needs met. As a result, he drove himself to make money and succeed in his work. This passion increased his worry, fretfulness, and fear about the future.

Jim experienced what many of us do: our passions regarding our work can be rooted in experiences or drives that have little to do with our actual jobs. We can approach our work being driven by the wrong motivations. The desire to succeed is godly. But being driven by fear or greed is not. During a particularly trying time when his work was not going well, he recognized his lack of joy and realized he wasn't trusting God with his work, his career, and his eventual retirement.

Jim repented and made a decision to trust God. When he did, peace came. He began to look to the future with hope. He began to study scriptures regarding trusting God and God's intention to supply His children's needs. He understood that he needed to do his part by working, managing his money well, and saving for retirement as he could. Beyond that, he realized he must trust the Lord for provision, and be at peace.

As men, we must realize that our work is more than just work. Our work is the arena in which God develops our lives. Viewing our work in this way changes our entire perspective and makes it far more meaningful. We should not shy away from our work or view it as something we have to do. We should embrace it and view it as a key place we will see God work in our lives.

Tested, Molded, and Blessed

In the book of Genesis, we read about the life of Joseph. At an early age, the Lord began to reveal Himself and His plan for Joseph through dreams. When Joseph told these dreams to his family, they were offended because the dreams related that he would be raised up into a high position above his family. In addition, because Joseph's father favored him over his older brothers, they became jealous of him. Their resentment led them to fake his death and sell him into slavery to get rid of him.

However, even as a slave in a foreign land, Joseph continued to trust God. He was diligent in all his duties and morally upright in all that he did. Regardless of where he was or what happened to him, his diligence and God's favor on his life led to him being promoted and put in charge. First, Joseph's master put him in charge of his entire household. Then, when he was falsely accused of adultery and thrown into prison, the chief jailor soon put him in charge of the prison. Eventually, his walk with God was recognized, and through an amazing chain of events Pharaoh appointed him governor over all Egypt.

Put yourself in Joseph's shoes. He was raised in a wealthy family. He was born and raised in a position of privilege. He was used to having servants attend to his family's needs and business. Now, all of a sudden, he is a slave and servant when he has done nothing wrong. He could have been bitter, resentful, wanting revenge, angry at his brothers for what they did to him, and angry at God for letting it all happen. It wasn't fair at all.

But that is not what Joseph did. Instead, he made a decision to work hard and be diligent, and to have integrity in all he did. He decided to trust God in his circumstances and to believe God knew where he was, understood that he had been treated unfairly, and would take care of him. Joseph did not know how it all would turn out. But he did choose to trust that God would bring to pass what He had shown to him about his future. He was a real man of faith.

Even though Joseph was falsely accused, imprisoned, and at times might have felt God had forgotten him, he persevered and worked diligently. God blessed him and raised him up to a position of prominence second only to Pharaoh. God was faithful and in His time raised Joseph up and fulfilled all He had put into Joseph's heart. In fact, He exceeded Joseph's expectations.

Every man should read about Joseph (Genesis 37, 39–50). We also need to study the life of David (in the books of Samuel and Chronicles), the life of Joshua (in the book of Joshua), and the life of Daniel (in the book of Daniel). These men were tried and tested. Their successes and failures are openly displayed, and the results of trusting God and choosing to please Him are shown. And there are other men, such as Jehoshaphat, Hezekiah, Josiah, Nehemiah, who are worth knowing about. They all experienced God shaping their characters and lives through their work.

By the way, none of these men were priests; they were all what we would call "secular leaders." They were not televangelists and they did not pastor large churches. But they were men who took their tasks seriously and they all had hearts for God. God raised them up and blessed them because they trusted Him and believed He would help them in their tasks. They all became exceptional leaders and had great influence on all around them.

Their work was blessed and they were blessed as they trusted God. Many became wealthy and prosperous. In the same way, God wants to bless our work and our lives. He wants to work in us and through us in our work life.

The Arena in Which God Develops Our Character

Our work is a great environment in which God can mold us. Whether in Joseph's time or today, in the workplace, men are exposed to various influences and temptations. They are tempted to scheme to get ahead, tempted in the area of sexual sin and adultery, tempted to lie to save their reputations or positions, tempted to steal or cheat to make money—and the list goes on. Either we live our faith and become godly men, or we compromise and face moral shipwreck.

The marketplace is a great place to practice character traits taught in the Bible. You can talk about your convictions, but the way you live them out is what people see. In the workplace, people look at who you are, what you do, how you do it, and your attitudes. They see your work ethic, your integrity, your attitudes toward others, and how you react under pressure. You can't hide these things. You can talk about being a Christian. But they want to see how you live your life.

Learning to work hard, to be honest in all our dealings, to achieve excellence in our profession, to practice discipline, to have balance in our lives, and to have courage are some of the things we must deal with in our work. Yes, we will be tested and at times feel defeated. We may face difficult work environments and pressure to compromise, lie, cheat, or be dishonest. These are tests of our character and challenges to our faith. Our relationship with God will either grow, diminish, or become stagnant. The pressures we face at work should drive us to God, cause us to study His Word, and practice what He leads us to do. When we do, we will change, and God will form His character in us.

A Lab Where We See God in Action

I see the workplace as God's laboratory where we learn how God's principles work practically. The workplace is real life, not theory. It's where we must learn to live out what we believe and gain wisdom as to how to do it. It's "where the rubber meets the road," as the saying goes.

In our work, we will have successes and defeats. Our ideals, our goals, and our dreams will be challenged at times; and at those times, our faith in God will be on the line. I've been blessed and betrayed, experienced financial prosperity, and almost lost it all because of bad decisions. It's been a real adventure. But God has always been faithful to His Word and has always provided for me and my family.

Our work is **where God has put us and where He wants to show Himself strong on our behalf.** There is an old and wise saying, "Bloom where you are planted." Look at your work through eyes of faith and see what God will do.

In my work, I have to make decisions involving millions of dollars. Buying land and developing it is an expensive business. There are some men that make decisions regarding billions of dollars in their businesses. Though I have always tried to act in integrity, I have made some bad business decisions.

I have never gotten up in the morning and said to myself, "I want to make some bad decisions today." But even though I have always wanted to make good decisions, I have admittedly made some bad choices or decisions at times. I've made some decisions that have cost me financially. In the hard aftermath of one of these times—after I stopped complaining and being disappointed in God for allowing this to happen—I realized I had a choice. I could give up, stay disappointed, stop trusting God, grow bitter, and become fearful that things would continue to go badly in the future. Or, I could determine to continue to trust God even though I didn't understand everything. I could pray, ask God for wisdom, learn from my circumstances, and move forward.

As I chose to do this and prayerfully move forward, understanding began to come: it was a test of my faith. God began to teach me and change my heart. I gained wisdom and understanding (great treasures). And, as I decided to trust Him in spite of my circumstances, things began to work out.

My good times have been more frequent than the bad or trying times. But we tend to remember the mistakes and hardship more than all of the blessings God has given us. We need to reverse that and cultivate a thankful heart for all of the good God has done for us. Even during the difficult times, He promises to provide for us as we seek Him. Having a joyful and thankful heart is a blessing to our life and it affects all those around us.

Yes, at times I have wanted to throw in the towel and have been discouraged. Like most, I have looked at my shortcomings and mistakes and wondered if I had what it took. But as I sought

God, I realized my hope was to be in him. Not myself. He is my hope and my future. I am imperfect, but He is not. He forgives, helps us, and leads us as we seek Him. When I am weak, He is strong. He is the friend that sticks closer than any brother and will never leave or forsake us. And, He has a great plan for each of us. He wants to help us and bless us.

Many men come to similar crossroads. We all have the same choice when things are difficult: give up, or trust God in spite of our temporary lack of understanding of why things aren't working. And it is temporary. God promises to give us wisdom when we ask for it. If we cry out to God, He will answer us—not always as we expect or think, but according to His purposes and plan for us. As we come out from the crisis on the other end, because we have surrendered to Him and His will afresh and anew, we will be changed: more joyful, more peaceful, and with renewed purpose. We will have seen Him at work, being faithful to His word and promises.

A Place Where God Deals with Fear

Our work lives also bring ample opportunity for God to transform the way we deal with fear and uncertainty. In today's marketplace, there is diminishing certainty and security. We can expect our work life to be full of surprises and ups and downs, bringing opportunity for stress, doubt, confusion, and fear. God wants us to be able to have peace in the midst of whatever circumstances our work brings.

I am a home builder, and the downturns in the late 1980s and the great recession that began in 2006 devastated my industry and greatly affected Joan and me. I've spent a lot of time on my knees seeking God for His direction for my business and for solutions to the sometimes overwhelming problems. How were we to survive?

Should I change industries? How was I to make a living? These questions all became realities.

It's one thing to make bad decisions that cost you money. It's another to have the entire economy move against you and there seems to be nothing you can do. But take heart, God always has a plan. He is bigger than the economy and is not limited by what is happening around us.

The enemy wants to rob us of our peace and try to steal our trust in God. God wants to work through all of our life circumstances to draw us closer to Him and to make us more like His Son. *"Those whom he foreknew he also predestined to be conformed to the image of his Son, that his Son would be the firstborn among many brothers and sisters"* (Romans 8:29). One of the ways God does this "conforming" or "molding" is to get rid of the things that hinder us.

Fear is one of those things, because it keeps us from trusting God to accomplish all He wants to do through us. God wants us to learn to operate without giving in to fear. Knowing Him more and knowing His love for us overcomes fear. *"There is no fear in love, but perfect love drives out fear, because fear has to do with punishment. The one who fears punishment has not been perfected in love"* (1 John 4:18). We may still feel fear, but as we draw closer to Him it will lose its grip on us.

When my children were small, I used to throw them up in the air and catch them. (Luckily, I never dropped them!) At first, they were a bit taken aback. But after a while, they would ask me to throw them higher and higher. They loved it (I am not sure my wife did). They had confidence I wouldn't drop them. They trusted me.

The same is true with our relationship with our Heavenly Father. He will lead us into situations in our workplaces where we will have to trust Him. As I was driven to my knees by the changes in my industry during the recession, I learned that God was always faithful. Our financial needs were met. What's more, as I sought God during these times, my heart changed, my priorities changed, my thinking changed, and my relationship with God grew. I began to see the truths of Scripture differently, and in some areas my doctrinal beliefs changed. I began to see God as more loving, caring, and close to me, and I became more compassionate and merciful (because I felt a need for those things personally). I grew in my relationship with God and, by the way, that is the most important thing.

Crisis changes us. It makes or breaks us. If we are being led by God, we learn He will take care of us through the risks and we will come out with the result He desires; often different than we thought. He allows us to experience fear, in order to teach us we have nothing to fear with Him. I am not saying we will get to the point where we will never fear again. We are human. But we can learn to cast the fear upon Him and to continue to choose to trust Him while we are walking through the circumstances. As we choose to trust Him, peace returns along with an assurance all will work out. Jesus said,

> *"Come unto me all you who are weary and burdened, and I will give you rest. Take my yoke upon you and learn from me, for I am gentle and humble in heart, and you will find rest for your souls. For my yoke is easy and my burden is light."* (Matthew 11:28-30)

Jesus said He is gentle and humble, not angry and unreachable. He said He will give us rest for our souls! Rest means peace and a sound mind! That is His desire for us. Though we mess up, though we are afraid, He is with us. He said He will never leave us or forsake us (Hebrews 13:5)!

God's Heart for Our Work

In the workplace, we are put to the test. At some point, our faith, our conduct, our character, and our purpose will be tested. Will we trust God and do what is pleasing to Him, or will we surrender to compromise?

As we learn to stand in faith, trust God, and surrender to His will, we will see Him work in our lives. As a result, our relationship with God and our faith in Him will grow.

God wants to work in our lives, and through our lives, in our work. He wants to change us, challenge us, reproduce the character and nature of Christ in us, and reveal Himself to us. He will do much of this in our workplace.

QUESTIONS FOR REFLECTION AND DISCUSSION

1. How has God developed you through your work? List below one or two jobs you have had, and how God worked in you during each one.

   _____

   _____

   _____

   _____

2. Have you been tested in your work to compromise negatively? What was the result? Write below some tests you have encountered in the marketplace and how you responded.

   _____

   _____

   _____

3. In light of what you have just read, have any of your thoughts or attitudes changed about your job? If so, how?

4. Do you currently see God active in your work? If so, how?

TAKE A KNEE

Let's pray: *"Father, I ask You to show me all You want to do in my life through my work. Show me if I have viewed my work in a manner that is unscriptural or unpleasing to You. I realize You use my work to develop my character. Develop my character into the man You want me to be. Help me to understand the work You are doing in me, that I may more fully cooperate. I invite You to work in my life and change me as needed. I ask You to bless my work and cause it to prosper. I trust You and welcome You to make me more Christlike."*

Chapter 3

LIFE ON THE JOB

Work has always been part of my life. In college, some of my friends' parents gave them a monthly allowance so they didn't have to work. Mine could not, as my dad was a pastor and money was limited. But since I had been working since I was fourteen, I didn't think much of it. I accepted it as part of life.

When Joan and I got married while I was still going to college, we both worked to make ends meet. Joan's dad died a few months prior to our getting married, my dad had just started a new church, and we had to make it on our own. Joan was a secretary at a business and I worked part time in a warehouse stocking shelves, packaging orders, and delivering them to customers. We were happy and in love, our basic needs were met, and we believed better years were ahead. The basic life lessons I'd learned about work as a young teen with my first jobs stood us well.

God ordained work—it is good for us and good for others. A strong work ethic is a vital building block of a society. The belief that hard work, diligence, and perseverance will pay off is critical for a society to grow, prosper, and build a strong economy.

It Is Normal to Work and Have a Job

We all need to work to provide for ourselves; working for ourselves or someone else is the normal way of life God set up for man. I fully realize some people are physically unable to work. But those are in the minority (and even many of those can do some type of work). And there are others whose crafts or professions do not lend themselves to typical jobs; even so, they can work to excel at what they do. A concert musician, for example, even if he does not have a job currently for his music, can still work diligently and practice his skill of being a musician. And if he has no music jobs, he should have another source of making money.

Only a lazy man chooses not to work when he could, and has no desire to be productive. Proverbs calls this type of man a *sluggard*. *"The sluggard will not plow because of winter; therefore he will beg during the harvest and have nothing"* (Proverbs 20:4). Another word used for a lazy man is *slothful*. Several scriptures refer to laziness, including Proverbs 6:6-11, 13:4, 15:19, 19:24, 21:25, and 22:13. Clearly, being lazy is not an option for a Christian man.

There is a difference between a man who can work and won't, and a man who wants to work and can't. Men who want to work but cannot may become discouraged or depressed because they cannot be productive and provide for themselves and their families. Those who are disabled may also become discouraged, as they desire to be more productive. When the diligent man is out of work and can't find a job or can't work, he will usually be very frustrated. However, the lazy man is content not to work and to let others provide for him.

Webster's Dictionary defines *diligence* as "steady application in business of any kind; constant effort to accomplish what is undertaken; exertion of body or mind without unnecessary delay or sloth; due attention; industrious; attentive." Many scriptures praise diligent work and the rewards associated with it:

> *The slothful man does not roast what he took in hunting, but diligence is man's precious possession. (Proverbs 14:27)*
>
> *Do you see a man who excels in his work? He will stand before kings; He will not stand before unknown men. (Proverbs 22:29; see also Proverbs 10:4; 12:11-14; 14:23; Ezra 5:8; Romans 12:80)*

With that in mind, let's talk of some basic truths regarding work that we should all embrace.

Practical Work Matters

The following practical points are good things not only to believe and practice yourself, but to teach your children, if you are a father.

Do the job you can.

If you don't have work, your job is to find a job or work to do. You can spend eight hours a day looking for a job through different sources, seeking the Lord, or doing temp work. I've been unemployed and know how discouraging and draining it can be. The work you do to find a job can be some of the hardest you can do mentally and emotionally.

If you are young and just starting out, can't get your ideal job, or have to start below the level you want or think you are qualified for, then get what you can. Begin to work and earn money. You can look for a better position as you can or advance over time. Know that all work is valuable and benefits others. As we practice diligence, faithfulness, having a good attitude, and doing the best job we can, we can believe God to bless our work.

Let's look at the example of Joseph in the book of Genesis again. He came from a wealthy family with servants and much privilege. He was sold into slavery by his own brothers and became a slave. He was falsely accused by his master's wife and then became a prisoner in a jail. Things seemed to go from bad to worse. He could have said, "I tried to honor God and did what was right and now my situation has only worsened. Where is God is all of this?" If anyone had a reason to complain, it was Joseph.

He deserved none of the treatment he received, yet he continued to be diligent in all areas of his life and gained favor. He continued to trust God for the final outcome. Guess what, he won! At the proper time, God elevated him to a place of great privilege and rank in Egypt. God had been preparing him for the purpose and plan He had for him. He built into Joseph the character he needed to be an effective ruler and not be caught up in pride.

Practice being a good employee.

No matter what work we do, we need to apply ourselves to the task of being a good employee (even if you work for yourself). Be on time. Always do your best work. Be the person the boss can count on to get things done, and do it well. As a boss myself, I highly value the employees who are not only good at their jobs, but who actually make the entire workplace better through their work and attitudes.

We should also desire to have a good attitude toward everyone in our workplaces. No one likes to work with a contentious and critical person, or one with a sour disposition. We should encourage those around us and be cheerful as we trust God to help us and bless our work. Our life, mode of work, conscientiousness, diligence, and attitude will be a positive witness to all around us. Who we are and how we conduct ourselves is a great part of our ministry.

Think of the type of person you would want to work for you—or the type of people you would want to deal with in a company you were doing business with. You would want them to be cheerful, positive, knowledgeable, helpful, concerned about you and your needs, attentive, and honest. We all want to deal with those people, so we should all try to be that person.

Improve your skills.

As Christians, we are to become as skilled and accomplished in our work as we can, without neglecting our families or our personal relationship with God. *"Do you see a man who excels in his work? He will stand before kings; he will not stand before unknown men"* (Proverbs 22:29). We should strive to work to the best of our ability. Self-improvement is important, regardless of your type of work. Be as good at your job area as you can. Grow, improve, and excel.

Over the years, I have been privileged to work for men more knowledgeable than I, or more mature than I. I look back at how my life benefitted from them. I learned not only skills and technical knowledge, but how to treat people and the correct attitudes I should have. I worked for a man for a number of years who at times micro-managed me. I did not always like it, but I also learned a great deal from him as he challenged me to be better at my work and to work at a higher standard. I have also gained from other's counsel when I needed it.

Remember, you will gain a reputation for both the quality and quantity of your work. I have had employees who did excellent work but only accomplished 50 to 70% of the work others did. They were very conscientious, but did not get enough done. You will sometimes find a tension between working quickly and working with excellence. Some tasks take longer due to the nature of the work. Rushing can lead to error and, in some cases, bring results that can impact others negatively. Try to do quality work and to get as much accomplished as you can with the time you have. As you practice this, you will get better at it.

Accept the authority of your boss.

There are no perfect bosses (guess what, you're not perfect either!). But you can try to honor them and submit to their authority.* As a Christian, you cannot follow your boss's leadership or instruction to do anything illegal, unethical, immoral or unscriptural. But you can be a great employee and honor the one you work for, even though he or she is not perfect.

Resist peer pressure.

On the job, it's important to resist peer pressure to have bad attitudes or do things you know are wrong. You may have coworkers who will be critical, gossips, slanderers, or lazy in their work habits. It is easy to join them in finding faults in others or your

---

*For more on this topic, see the study in the Living Life God's Way series entitled *A Man and Authority*, by Lou Turner.

boss and become critical, but don't. Resist the temptation. It isn't honoring to the Lord and not a good example. Rather, let your example speak to them of the standards you believe in.

You can see a situation for what it is and not have a bad attitude, even when things are going badly. Act with honesty and integrity in all you do. Your presence should bring the level of work and attitudes up, not down. There are times that it may be necessary to take positive steps to correct negative things when the situation calls for it. You can take drastic steps in the midst of adverse circumstances, and do it because it is the right thing to do, not because you have malice in your heart toward others.

Don't be a workaholic.

There is a time to work and a time to stop. If you have a wife or family, your work, while important, is not as important as your wife and children. You may spend more hours at work in a typical day than at home with them, but in your heart they take precedence.

Don't let your job become more important than them. If you neglect your family, it will have consequences. Give them the time they deserve and need. You are needed at home to be the husband and father they need. Your wife needs time with you, as do your children.

Remember, you are not your job. You are God's child and your identity is more than your job. You can work hard, be focused, and still set aside time for other priorities.

God at Work

Our perspective regarding work is very important. Our work can be just work, or it can be part of our relationship with God. Since His Spirit is in us, God wants to be intimately involved in every aspect of our lives, including our work. When we begin to realize that, our daily efforts will take on an entirely different dimension. We will see our work as an expression of our life, and God's life in us. It is no longer just work or a job, but part of who we are and what we do.

Work is not something we have to do, it is something we get to do. Work that is blessed of God is to be desired and something to be thankful for. Rather than futility, it can bring purpose and fulfillment in life when approached in faith.

Yes, there will be difficulties and trials in life. But these are opportunities to grow and see God work in us and through us. Adversity and trials can lead to opportunities and rewards. Take them on in faith, trusting God to help you and be with you.

QUESTIONS FOR REFLECTION AND DISCUSSION

1. If you are employed, how do you honestly view your job? What is positive about it? Negative?

   _____

   _____

   _____

   _____

2. If, for some reason, you are unemployed, what do you view as your daily work?

   _____

   _____

   _____

   _____

3. What kind of attitude do you bring to your workplace? What kind of attitude do you have toward those you work with? Write your answer below.

_____

_____

_____

_____

4. After finishing the last three chapters regarding work, is there a way you'd like to change your approach to work in general or your job in particular? If so, write below how you can do that.

_____

_____

_____

_____

TAKE A KNEE

Let's pray: *"Father, help me to see my work as a platform to provide for myself and to influence others. Help me to be Your light in my workplace and help me to excel in my work. Show me how to be a better worker and bless those around me. I want to excel in my work and do as well as I can. Put in me Your desire to be a diligent worker. Teach me the things you are wanting to teach me and give me 'eyes to see' and 'ears to hear' what you are wanting to say to me and show me. Help me to work in faith for You."*

Chapter 4
A Man's Work Is Integral to His Ministry

Just after God liberated His people from slavery in Egypt, God spoke to Moses and gave him a message to tell all Israel:

> Now therefore, if you will indeed obey My voice and keep My covenant, then you shall be a special treasure to Me above all people: for all the earth is Mine. And you shall be to Me a kingdom of priests and a holy nation. These are the words which you shall speak to the children of Israel. (Exodus 19:5-6)

God intended Israel to be a kingdom of priests. All would be speaking the truth of His Word, living their lives for Him, teaching their children His ways, and displaying His truth to the world. They were to live as God's chosen people; in turn, He would greatly bless them.

The Apostle Peter was speaking of New Testament believers when he said,

> *But you are a chosen generation, a royal priesthood, a holy nation, His own special people, that you may proclaim the praises of Him who called you out of darkness into His marvelous light; who were once not a people but are now the people of God, who had not obtained mercy but now have obtained mercy. (1 Peter 2:9-10)*

God intends for all Christians to be His priests, or ministers. As Christians we are called, chosen, redeemed, and placed where we are for a purpose—God's purpose. He desires to reveal Himself to the world through us.

Over my work life, God has led me into various positions. I have been both a full-time pastor and worked in the corporate world. I had to come to see that God did not view my work as a pastor as more valuable than my work as an executive in the marketplace. I was in ministry no matter what work I was doing. I was His minister wherever I was or whatever I was doing.

Unfortunately, many men have not come to realize that. They go to church to be ministered to, and see that as their spiritual service to God. Then they go to their jobs and do "non-spiritual" work. They look to pastors as the ministers and priests, and see them as somehow different from themselves. They do not consider that their normal work lives are an integral part of their God-given ministry.

Misconceptions about Ministry

This idea is strengthened by how we use the words "minister" and "layman." If you ask most people to define "ministry," they will speak of pastors teaching in the pulpit or someone on a church's pastoral staff. Many men believe that since they have not "arrived" into a position on staff in church ministry, they are merely laymen, and God does not expect much from them. After all, they are not "called into the ministry."

They, like many people, think that being "in ministry" means working on a church staff or being in a full-time vocational ministry position. However, in churches large enough to have a staff, few staff members teach the Word of God to the congregation or do the work we typically think of when we think of being "in the ministry." Many, if not most, people on church staff lead various program areas or do some type of administrative work.

I have personally counseled some of these people and have employed some who had previously been in church staff positions. It is surprising how many were either disappointed or disillusioned by their experiences. They didn't feel they were any more involved in personal ministry than when they were "laymen." They went into their church staff position hoping they would be more involved in "ministry" and became disappointed that what they hoped for was not what they experienced. The Church, like any organization, needs people who are talented to accomplish its tasks, much of which is administrative in nature.

"Laymen" is one of the most damaging words used in the church. It is often used to differentiate between full-time or vocational ministers and people who earn a living in the marketplace. This somehow puts the ministries of full-time pastors as a higher calling or position than the ministries of other men.

Yet the word "layman" is not found in the New Testament. It is only found in the Old Testament and comes from the Hebrew word *zur*, which means to be a stranger, foreigner, or outsider. It was used to describe anyone who was not the "High Priest." There was only one High Priest in Israel at a time, so everyone else was a layman. The High Priest was a symbolic position of the coming

Messiah, Jesus Christ, who is the High Priest today of the Church worldwide. He is the true High Priest.

The High Priest of the Old Testament was from the tribe of Levi and was the chief priest. The Levites were to be a priestly tribe and teach all Israel the ways of God. But only Aaron and his descendant sons could share in the office of the High Priest.

Thus, all of the other Levites were considered "laymen" as they could not become priests in the way Aaron's direct descendants could. And the rest of the Israelites were all "laymen." So, by pure definition, any of us today who can't trace our lineage to Aaron are laymen, including our pastors and others in vocational ministry.

When Christ died and rose again, the role of priests being descended from Aaron was done away with. All believers became "priests" or ministers. While God calls some to work in vocational ministry, the percentage is less than one percent of all believers. All other believers are called to be out in the world as Christ's representatives, living for Him and reaching the world. There are no longer any "laymen." We are all called and chosen as His ministers. There is no scriptural basis in the New Testament for "laymen." As it says in 1 Peter 2: 9-10, we are called to be a "royal priesthood." We, all Christians, are called to be His ministers and His priests.

Challenged to Minister

We as men, need to be challenged. We need to be stretched to reach and achieve. We need to be taught the truth to set us free to become the men God intends us to be.

Effective pastors will raise up men mighty in spirit, with a passion to do God's work and will in their lives—who see their lives as an adventure with God, full of challenges and opportunity.

A MAN'S WORK IS INTEGRAL TO HIS MINISTRY

Pastors should challenge their congregation to believe God to be real in their lives in their work and in their calling.

Christian men are not laymen; they are God's priests and ministers. They may not act like it now, but that is God's intention.

> *The Spirit Himself bears witness with our spirit that we are children of God, and if children, then heirs of God and joint heirs with Christ, if indeed we suffer with Him that we may also be glorified together. (Romans 8:16-17)*

> *For you are all sons of God through faith in Christ Jesus. For as many of you as were baptized into Christ have put on Christ. There is neither Jew nor Greek, there is neither slave nor free, there is neither male nor female, for you are all one in Christ Jesus. And if you are Christ's, then you are Abraham's seed, and heirs according to the promise. (Galatians 3:26-29)*

As believers, we are heirs of God, joint heirs with Christ. No one is more "heir" than another. We cannot hide behind our pastors and leave God's work to them. We must all be about our Father's work. We all have access to Him, and through His Spirit we are to perform the works spoken of in the Bible as God leads us.

What *Is* Ministry?

So what is a man's ministry? Let's look at the word "ministry" both as a noun, as in "a minister," and a verb, as in "to minister."

First the noun. According to Webster, a minister is "a chief servant, an agent appointed to carry out the affairs of the one he serves." A minister is also a delegate, an ambassador, or a representative. In the New Testament, several Greek words are translated "minister." One is *diakonos,* a word that means "a servant."

So, **a minister is a delegate or representative of one in authority over him, serving him to carry out his desires.** What a great definition of a Christian! We are all called to be God's representatives, His ambassadors, to serve Him and carry out His desires and plans. We are His ministers. He wants to work through us to accomplish His purposes.

Now let's look at the verb. Webster says "to minister" means, "to supply a need, to attend to or serve, to give things needed." So, we minister to others when we meet their needs, whether physical, spiritual, emotional, financial, or practical.

Jesus told a parable about a man who typified ministry. We call him the "Good Samaritan" (see Luke 10:29-37). In this parable, a man left Jerusalem and travelled to Jericho. On the way, thieves attacked and beat him, leaving him for dead. Three men came along and saw him. First came a priest, who crossed to the other side of the road. He didn't want to get involved or dirty his hands. Second, a Levite passed by. He likewise chose to pass by on the other side of the road. His attitude was that surely the man on the road was "unclean" and unworthy to touch or help. His sin must have led to his circumstances. After all, he was a priest and did not want to stoop to help this obviously undeserving man.

Lastly, a man from Samaria came along. This man stopped and had compassion on the beaten man. He bandaged him, put the man on his own animal, and took him to an inn where he gave the innkeeper some money and told him to take care of the traveler so he could recover. The Samaritan also stated that if, when he returned, the expenses for the man's care exceeded the amount he had given to the innkeeper, he would take care of it.

Now, who ministered to the man? It is interesting that Jesus stated a Samaritan took care of the man. The Jews despised the people from Samaria because they had intermarried with non-Jews. They were looked upon as "less than." The Samaritans knew this. Yet this despised man acted as God's minister when the supposedly righteous priest and the Levite did not. It's as if a worship leader came along and saw him, and sang a worship song and left. Or if a teacher or preacher came along and preached a sermon to him and left. That was not his need; left alone and not tended to, the man would have died. He needed help to stay alive physically. The man who ministered to his need was God's minister in that circumstance. He gave life-giving care, compassion, and love.

So, true ministry is meeting others' needs, whatever they are. Jesus said in Mark 9:41 (NKJV), *"For whoever gives you a cup of water to drink in My name, because you belong to Christ, assuredly, I say to you, he will by no means lose his reward."* Jesus died to save people. Wherever He went, He ministered to people's needs, both physically and spiritually. As God's delegates, His ministers, we are called to serve Him and be a channel He can work through. That is ministry, and we are all equally called to do this.

What types of things does a minister do? There are many actions that minister:

- Giving your money
- Giving your time and effort
- Encouraging people or supporting their heart needs
- Praying for others
- Serving others or caring for their practical needs
- Teaching or speaking Scripture to others
- Sharing the salvation message to others
- Helping others

The list could go on; the opportunities are all around us.

One day, I was outside in my front yard when I saw my neighbor across the street on crutches. I went over to ask him what had happened. He told me that because of an injury he had an infection in the bone of his foot and the doctors told him he could lose his foot. He was quite concerned. I asked him if I could pray for him, and he said yes. So, there in the middle of the street I prayed for God to heal his foot and to reveal Himself to him. After I prayed, he told me no one had ever prayed for him before. After that, every time he saw me, he said "Keep praying." I told him I would. He didn't lose his foot and I gained a friend. I was God's minister to him for his need.

Our words, attitudes, and behavior can have a profound effect on those around us. Our actions can speak volumes when someone may not be open to our words. It can be the thing that does open them to the gospel.

Here are just a few examples of what marketplace ministry looks like in action:

A young man's blessing. While I worked in the oil industry, I was on my way back from a business trip when I decided to stop and check out a development on a lake that I had passed several times. As I entered the sales center, a young man came up to me and asked if he could help me. He began to answer my questions and tell me about the development. I sensed he was a Christian. As we talked, he sensed I was concerned about a number of things. When I was about to leave, he laid his hand on my shoulder and said, "The Lord's peace be upon you." Immediately I felt peace go through my being. His simple act truly ministered to me. I have never forgotten that. He probably was not aware of how that simple act ministered to my soul and spirit.

An attorney's compassion. Another time, I met a Christian man who told me he was a divorce attorney. I asked him how, as a Christian, he could be in that role. He related to me that when people come to him they often are hurting and looking for counsel and comfort. They are open to ministry. He has led over 150 people to Christ in his office. Not bad for a divorce attorney. Though he personally was not in favor of divorce, he gained many opportunities to speak the truth to others and pray with them.

A business owner's passion. I know a man who owns his own small company. He has a passion for reaching out to men. He can relate to them and has true compassion for them. He is constantly starting men's groups to minister and encourage men. Some of his groups have grown to 40 or 50 men. He knows he is God's minister in the marketplace. He reaches men no pastor ever will.

Our entire lives are filled with opportunities to minister. We can influence countless lives as we go about our calling as God's men or women in the workplace, and reach people pastors can never reach.

Being Available to God for Ministry

We need to put some "feet" to our being God's priest or minister. It begins with surrendering to God in our hearts to be His minister, and then beginning to make ourselves available. Below are some practical steps we can take daily.

1. *Ask God to use you today.* Asking God to use you makes His heart glad. Deciding to make ourselves available and praying for Him to use you daily will increase the opportunities for ministry.
2. *Look for opportunity.* Being aware of our surroundings and the people we come into contact with can make us aware of opportunities to reach out to others. A sick neighbor gives the opportunity to take food and show concern. A troubled coworker gives the opportunity to be a friend, and give wise counsel. A friend in troubled financial times can prompt a phone call to show concern and pray. If we are aware and sensitive to those around us, God will prompt us to reach out.
3. *Obey the Holy Spirit's leading.* When opportunities come, we often shrink back out of fear of rejection or feelings of inadequacy. This keeps God from using us and deprives us of the joy of being involved with what God is doing. The enemy wants to

keep us from reaching out and helping others. We have to walk through this fear and simply determine to do what we are able to do. By the way, God only uses *imperfect* people.
4. *Pray over the ministry areas already available to you.* Our wives, our families, our church friends, our work, our neighbors, and those we have contact with are a daily opportunity for us to make a positive impact. Our everyday lives will provide opportunities for ministry.

Remember, you are God's representative here on Earth. As you go about your work, God will use your example, your character, your actions, and your words to minister and reach others. We just need to make ourselves available to Him to work through.

Most of us live in a neighborhood, surrounded by neighbors. We should all see our neighborhoods as places where we can reach out and minister to those around us. One great way is to prayer walk our neighborhoods and pray over our neighbors as we walk. We can pray for God to provide opportunities for us to reach out to them and minister to them, and for them to turn to Him in faith.

Every Man a Minister

We simply must change our thinking about ministry and get back to what ministry actually is. The church is called to equip us, the believers and saints, for ministry. The Bible refers to all true believers as saints. We may not always act like it, but in God's eyes we are. The Bible says we are called, chosen, and are joint heirs with Christ. We are partakers of salvation, God's Spirit dwells in us and God wants to work through us. We are His ministers to the world . . . PRAISE GOD! Not because we deserve it, but because we have been washed in Christ's blood and our sins have been washed away. We have been made white as snow and our sins have been removed from us as far as the East is from the West. We are blessed to be a blessing!

God gave His Holy Spirit to all believers, not just some called to vocational ministry. His Spirit lives in you to prompt you, empower you, lead you, and work through you. The promises given by God to His children were for *all* of His children, not just some of them. The enemy wants us to believe we are just "laymen" and are not qualified to minister. Don't believe that. You are God's called and chosen.

God has no second-class men. He measures us by our faithfulness to His calling, wherever that may be. God's Word can live in us wherever we are. We can accomplish mighty acts for God in our work. We can be men of strong faith in any position and become "mighty in spirit" in any place. There are times the way we live our life is ministering to others. At other times, we need to use words and speak life and truth to others.

Being in God's Word

God tells us in the Bible that we are to study the Word to have our mind renewed and to come into agreement with Him. It is only by reading and studying His Word that we can know His will for us and how we are supposed to live our lives:

> *"Do not be conformed to this world, but be transformed by the renewal of your mind, that by testing you may discern what is the will of God, and what is good and acceptable and perfect." (Romans 12:2)*

> *"Do your best to present yourself to God as one approved, a worker who has no need to be ashamed, rightly handling the Word of truth." (2 Timothy 2:15)*

Scripture is clear that as God's children and priests, we need to study His Word and apply it to our life. I often hear from men that they do not like to read. I tell them that, at one time, I did not like to read either. But as I started reading and thinking about the Bible, I wanted to do it more. I now enjoy reading and look forward to it. I have learned a great deal from anointed writers and teachers of God's Word by reading their books. I have also learned a great deal from God's Holy Spirit as I read His Word and He teaches me directly.

Before I start reading, I always pray that God will bless me as I read and give me understanding. Sometimes I pray over the meaning of each verse, asking God to make it real in my life. The Bible blesses my life and gives me instruction, correction, and inspiration as I read it. Do I always understand everything I read? No. But I know I can ask God for understanding of difficult verses and move on. Often, I gain understanding later as I study and think on it. The Holy Spirit gives me understanding.

Yes, there are times I have to exercise discipline and do my reading and prayer when I feel I need to do other things and really don't have a great desire to do so. But I am always thankful when I spend time in the Word. If I have to rush off and get to other things, I can spend time with the Lord later in the day. Obviously, I can pray over my day as I go and seek His presence in the midst of my work. Regardless, I have a great need for Him, even after many years of seeking Him. The Bible never loses its power to speak to me and gives me guidance in my everyday life.

Seeking God through prayer and Bible study is not just a good idea; it is vitally important. We all need to develop the discipline of setting aside time for it. We can get up early or do it later in the day. But developing the discipline of seeking Him is vital to our life. It will give us guidance, direction, wisdom, and understanding as we go through life. It will keep us from making bad decisions and mistakes that can hurt us, hinder our life, and affect our family and work.

Seek the Lord, get godly men to seek their counsel around you, and practice the truths of God's Word.

Some Examples of Ministry in the Bible

Philip was a deacon of the church at Jerusalem. He was among those scattered from Jerusalem by the persecution of the church. He went to Samaria (the center of false religion and of those who had broken away from Israel and followed false gods) and proclaimed the gospel. He healed the sick, cast out demons, and demonstrated the power of God through the Holy Spirit in him. Many in the city accepted Christ, and the Bible states that there was much joy in the city because of all he said and did (see Acts 8:4–8).

After he ministered in Samaria, Philip was led to go down a road where he encountered a man who was a court official to a queen. This man was reading the book of Isaiah from a scroll. He was studying a passage about Christ, but he did not understand what he was reading. The Holy Spirit told Philip to go over to the man and join him. The Bible says Philip ran over to him and heard him reading Isaiah. He asked the man if he understood what he was reading. The man said no, and Philip explained the Scripture to him. The man accepted Christ and Philip baptized him. He was then translated by God to another city where he continued to proclaim the gospel (see Acts 8:26–40).

Paul, in all of his writings in the New Testament, encouraged believers to seek God and do the work God was leading them to do. Paul, after having his experience on the Damascus road and accepting Christ, was made temporarily blind. The Holy Spirit spoke to a man called Ananias, who is simply described as a disciple of Christ. He told him to go to the house where Paul was staying and pray for Paul to regain his sight, lead him to be baptized in the Holy Spirit, and baptize him in water. Ananias obeyed the Lord and did these things. He was not a leader in the church, but a believer who obeyed the Lord.

The Lord is looking for those who are available to Him and willing to obey Him. He will work through any believer who is willing to obey Him and be a channel for Him to work through. The more time we spend seeking Him and being in His Word, the more sure we will be of the work He wants us to do. As we obey Him, He will work through us.

So, do you want to do the works of God? Seek Him, obey Him, and trust Him, and He will work through you. God works through people and is looking for those He can work through.

QUESTIONS FOR REFLECTION AND DISCUSSION

1. Do you believe God wants to work through you?

2. Do you believe God wants to work through all believers to do His work?

A MAN'S WORK IS INTEGRAL TO HIS MINISTRY

3. What do you think might be hindering God from working through you as He wants to?

_____

_____

_____

_____

4. Think about how you could "preach" the gospel through your life at work. List below how you see yourself ministering to others.

_____

_____

_____

_____

TAKE A KNEE

Let's pray: *"Father, I want to do the works you desire me to do. Please work through me and show me anything that is hindering You from doing Your works through me. I know You love me and want to use me. Draw me to You in prayer and Bible study daily, and speak to me as I seek you each day."*

A FINAL WORD

All men should see themselves as God's ministers. They are ministers to their wives, their families, their churches, their neighbors, and those around them in the workplace. We are to be God's full-time ministers wherever we are, as we strive to honor God in all aspects of our lives.

One famous Christian leader stated, "Preach the gospel at all times. And if necessary, use words." Our lives at work should show God's love, grace, truth, courage, joy, cheerfulness, diligence, and work ethic. And, when appropriate, we will have opportunities to speak the truth of God's Word to others.

Whatever we do for the Lord, in our work and ministry, it will bring a reward. Colossians 3:23-24 says,

> And whatever you do, do it heartily, as to the Lord and not to men, knowing that from the Lord you will receive the reward of the inheritance; for you serve the Lord Christ.

When we do our work as unto the Lord, we will see it in an entirely different light. Our motivation changes to please Him, not men. We will then work in integrity, committing ourselves to Him in our work. We believe that the reward for our work ultimately comes from Him. We do not have to labor hoping only in ourselves and the results of our work. We can work with joy, faith, and hope that He will help us and reward us in all we do.

ABOUT THE AUTHOR

Lou Turner wrote *Living Life God's Way* out of his passion for men to discover God, and to get to know Him and what He has for them. This 13-book men's discipleship series is the culmination of Lou's own journey—a life of seeking God, studying His Word, memorizing Scripture and meditating on it, and practical experience with family, community, marketplace work, and Christian ministry. It also comes, by Lou's own admission, from life experiences of both successes and mistakes, as a result of both good and bad decisions.

Lou has headed ministries, written and taught workshops, classes, and seminars, and discipled dozens of men. Now, he has put into print the things he has learned to help other men along their path and journey.

Most of Lou's growing up years were spent in Detroit and its suburbs, where he was raised in a pastor's home. Following his graduation from university with a Bachelor of Science in Business Administration, Lou and his wife planted and pastored a church for three years. After that time, he felt the strong call of God to return to business.

Over the years, Lou has served in numerous senior executive positions with national and international companies in the real estate and oil and gas industries. As of this writing, Lou is still active in business with his own home building company. He has

ABOUT THE AUTHOR

been married to his wife Joan since they were 20. They have three children and 10 grandchildren and make their home in Phoenix, Arizona.

www.ingramcontent.com/pod-product-compliance
Lightning Source LLC
Chambersburg PA
CBHW060412080526
44583CB00012B/539